A PAPER ZOO

A
Paper Zoo

A Collection of Animal Poems
by Modern American Poets

Selected by
RENÉE KAROL WEISS

Pictures by
ELLEN RASKIN

MACMILLAN PUBLISHING COMPANY
New York

Macmillan Publishing Company, 866 Third Avenue, New York, NY 10022. Collier Macmillan Canada, Inc. First published 1968; reissued 1987. Printed in the United States of America.
10 9 8 7 6 5 4 3 2 1
Library of Congress Cataloging-in-Publication Data. A Paper zoo. Summary: A collection of animal poems by well-known poets about such things as naming cats, a singing bird, and a slow-moving sloth. 1. Animals—Juvenile poetry. 2. Children's poetry, American. 3. American poetry—20th century. [1. Animals—Poetry. 2. American poetry—Collections] I. Weiss, Renée Karol. II. Raskin, Ellen, ill.
PS595.A5P3   1987   811'.54'08036   86-21733   ISBN 0-02-792750-4

For permission to include the following copyrighted selections, we are grateful to: Atlantic-Little, Brown and Co. for "The Snake" by Emily Dickinson; "The Waltzer in the House" by Stanley Kunitz (from his *Selected Poems 1928–1958*), copyright 1951, © 1958 by Stanley Kunitz, originally appeared in *The New Yorker*; "Lion" by William Jay Smith (from his *Poems 1947–1957*), copyright © 1956, 1957 by William Jay Smith. Doubleday & Company, Inc., for "The Sloth" by Theodore Roethke (from his *Words for the Wind*), copyright 1950 by Theodore Roethke. Donald Finkel for his "Hunting Song," copyright © 1959 by Donald Finkel. Harcourt Brace Jovanovich, Inc., for "now (more near ourselves than we)" by E. E. Cummings (from his *Complete Poems 1913–1962*), copyright © 1958 by E. E. Cummings. Harcourt Brace Jovanovich, Inc., and Faber and Faber Ltd for "'The Naming of Cats" by T. S. Eliot (from his *Old Possum's Book of Practical Cats*), copyright 1939 by T. S. Eliot, renewed 1967 by Esme Valerie Eliot. Henry Holt and Company for "Fireflies in the Garden" by Robert Frost (from *The Poetry of Robert Frost*, edited by Edward Connery Latham), copyright 1928, © 1969 by Holt, Rinehart and Winston, copyright © 1956 by Robert Frost. Alfred A. Knopf, Inc., for "Little Boy Blue" by John Crowe Ransom (from his *Two Gentlemen in Bonds*), copyright 1927 by Alfred A. Knopf, Inc., renewed 1955 by John Crowe Ransom; "Ploughing on Sunday" by Wallace Stevens (from *The Collected Poems of Wallace Stevens*), copyright 1923, renewed 1951 by Wallace Stevens. Macmillan Publishing Company for "Bats" by Randall Jarrell (from his *The Bat-Poet*), copyright © 1963, 1964 by Macmillan Publishing Company. New Directions Publishing Corporation for "The Magical Mouse" by Kenneth Patchen (from his *When We Were Together*), copyright 1952 by Kenneth Patchen; "The Horse" by William Carlos Williams (from his *Collected Later Poems*), copyright © 1944, 1963 by William Carlos Williams. The Swallow Press, Inc., for "To Be Sung by a Small Boy" by Yvor Winters (from his *Collected Poems*). Viking Penguin Inc. for "A Jelly-Fish" by Marianne Moore (from *The Complete Poems of Marianne Moore*), copyright © 1959 by Marianne Moore. Theodore Weiss for his "A Magic Carpet," copyright © 1968 by Theodore Weiss.

CONTENTS

A PAPER ZOO

E. E. Cummings

now (more near ourselves than we)
is a bird singing in a tree,
who never sings the same thing twice
and still that singing's always his

eyes can feel but ears may see
there never lived a gayer he;
if earth and sky should break in two
he'd make them one (his song's so true)

who sings for us for you for me
for each leaf newer than can be:
and for his own (his love) his dear
he sings till everywhere is here

9

Theodore Roethke

THE SLOTH

In moving-slow he has no Peer,
You ask him something in his Ear;
He thinks about it for a Year;

And, then, before he says a Word
There, upside down (unlike a Bird),
He will assume that you have Heard—

A most Ex-as-per-at-ing Lug.
But should you call his manner Smug,
He'll sigh and give his Branch a Hug;

Then off again to Sleep he goes,
Still swaying gently by his Toes,
And you just *know* he knows he knows.

THE SNAKE   *Emily Dickinson*

A narrow fellow in the grass
Occasionally rides;
You may have met him,—did you not?
His notice sudden is.

The grass divides as with a comb,
A spotted shaft is seen;
And then it closes at your feet
And opens further on.

He likes a boggy acre,
A floor too cool for corn.
Yet when a child, and barefoot,
I more than once, at morn,

Have passed, I thought, a whip-lash
Unbraiding in the sun, —
When, stooping to secure it,
It wrinkled, and was gone.

Several of nature's people
I know, and they know me;
I feel for them a transport
Of cordiality;

But never met this fellow,
Attended or alone,
Without a tighter breathing,
And zero at the bone.

Kenneth Patchen

THE MAGICAL MOUSE

I am the magical mouse
I don't eat cheese
I eat sunsets
And the tops of trees

I don't wear fur

I wear funnels
Of lost ships and the weather
That's under dead leaves
I am the magical mouse

I don't fear cats

Or woodsowls
I do as I please
Always
I don't eat crusts
I am the magical mouse
I eat
Little birds and maidens

That taste like dust

T. S. Eliot

THE NAMING OF CATS

The Naming of Cats is a difficult matter,
   It isn't just one of your holiday games;
You may think at first I'm as mad as a hatter
When I tell you, a cat must have THREE DIFFERENT NAMES.
First of all, there's the name that the family use daily,
   Such as Peter, Augustus, Alonzo or James,
Such as Victor or Jonathan, George or Bill Bailey—
   All of them sensible everyday names.
There are fancier names if you think they sound sweeter,
   Some for the gentlemen, some for the dames:
Such as Plato, Admetus, Electra, Demeter—
   But all of them sensible everyday names.
But I tell you, a cat needs a name that's particular,
   A name that's peculiar, and more dignified,
Else how can he keep up his tail perpendicular,
   Or spread out his whiskers, or cherish his pride?
Of names of this kind, I can give you a quorum,
   Such as Munkustrap, Quaxo, or Coricopat,
Such as Bombalurina, or else Jellylorum—
   Names that never belong to more than one cat.
But above and beyond there's still one name left over,
   And that is the name that you never will guess;
The name that no human research can discover—
   But THE CAT HIMSELF KNOWS, and will never confess.
When you notice a cat in profound meditation,
   The reason, I tell you, is always the same:
His mind is engaged in a rapt contemplation
   Of the thought, of the thought, of the thought of his name:
      His ineffable effable
      Effanineffable
Deep and inscrutable singular Name.

William Jay Smith

LION

The lion, ruler over all the beasts,
Triumphant moves upon the grassy plain
With sun like gold upon his tawny brow
And dew like silver on his shaggy mane.

Into himself he draws the rolling thunder,
Beneath his flinty paw great boulders quake;
He will dispatch the mouse to burrow under,
The little deer to shiver in the brake.

He sets the fierce whip of each serpent lashing,
The tall giraffe brings humbly to his knees,
Awakes the sloth, and sends the wild boar crashing,
Wide-eyed monkeys chittering, through the trees.

He gazes down into the quiet river,
Parting the green bulrushes to behold
A sunflower-crown of amethyst and silver,
A royal coat of brushed and beaten gold.

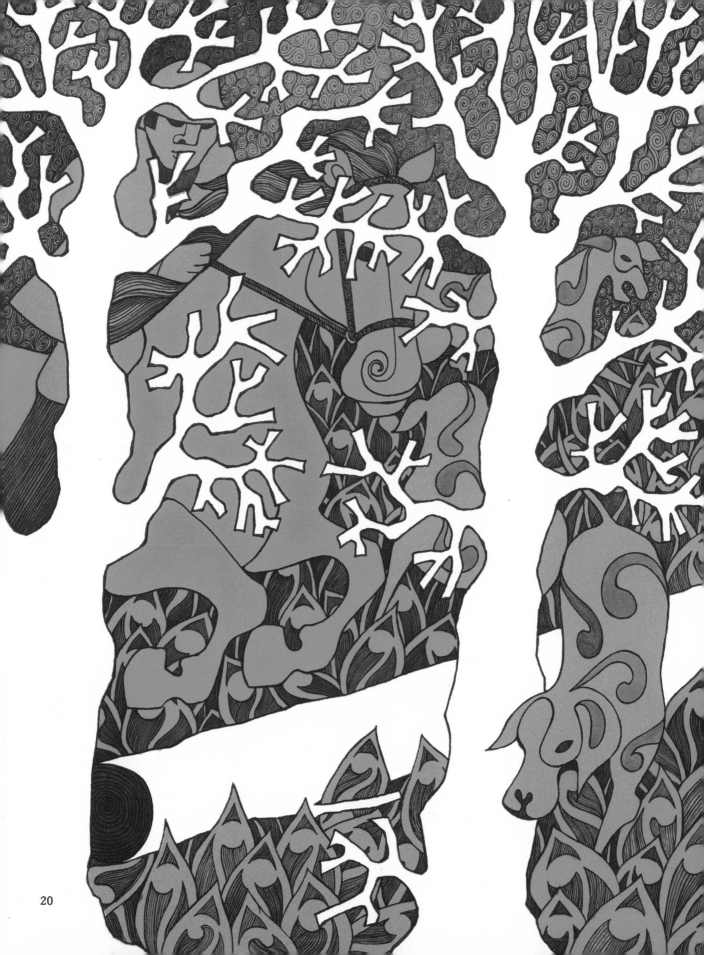

Donald Finkel

HUNTING SONG

The fox he came lolloping, lolloping,
Lolloping. His eyes were bright,
His ears were high.
He was like death at the end of a string
When he came to the hollow
Log. He ran in one side
And out of the other. O
He was sly.

The hounds they came tumbling, tumbling,
Tumbling. Their heads were low,
Their eyes were red.
The sound of their breath was louder than death
When they came to the hollow
Log. They boiled at one end
But a bitch found the scent. O
They were mad.

The hunter came galloping, galloping,
Galloping. All damp was his mare
From her hooves to her mane.
His coat and his mouth were redder than death
When he came to the hollow
Log. He took in the rein
And over he went. O
He was fine.

The log he just lay there, alone in
The clearing. No fox nor hound
Nor mounted man
Saw his black round eyes in their perfect disguise
(As the ends of a hollow
Log). He watched death go through him,
Around him and over him. O
He was wise.

21

Randall Jarrell

BATS

A bat is born
Naked and blind and pale.
His mother makes a pocket of her tail
And catches him. He clings to her long fur
By his thumbs and toes and teeth.
And then the mother dances through the night
Doubling and looping, soaring, somersaulting—
Her baby hangs on underneath.
All night, in happiness, she hunts and flies.
Her high sharp cries
Like shining needlepoints of sound
Go out into the night and, echoing back,
Tell her what they have touched.
She hears how far it is, how big it is,
Which way it's going:
She lives by hearing.
The mother eats the moths and gnats she catches
In full flight; in full flight
The mother drinks the water of the pond
She skims across. Her baby hangs on tight.
Her baby drinks the milk she makes him
In moonlight or starlight, in mid-air.
Their single shadow, printed on the moon
Or fluttering across the stars,
Whirls on all night; at daybreak
The tired mother flaps home to her rafter.
The others all are there.
They hang themselves up by their toes,
They wrap themselves in their brown wings.
Bunched upside-down, they sleep in air.
Their sharp ears, their sharp teeth, their quick sharp faces
Are dull and slow and mild.
All the bright day, as the mother sleeps,
She folds her wings about her sleeping child.

Marianne Moore

A JELLYFISH

Visible, invisible,
    a fluctuating charm
an amber-tinctured amethyst
    inhabits it, your arm
approaches and it opens
    and it closes; you had meant
to catch it and it quivers;
    you abandon your intent.

William Carlos Williams

THE HORSE

The horse moves
independently
without reference
to his load

He has eyes
like a woman and
turns them
about, throws

back his ears
and is generally
conscious of
the world. Yet

he pulls when
he must and
pulls well, blowing
fog from

his nostrils
like fumes from
the twin
exhausts of a car.

Yvor Winters

TO BE SUNG BY A SMALL BOY WHO HERDS GOATS

Sweeter than rough hair
On earth there is none:
Rough as the wind
And brown as the sun!

I toss high my short arms,
Brown as the sun!
I creep on the mountains
And never am done!

Sharp-hoofed, hard-eyed,
Trample on the sun!
Sharp ears, stiff as wind,
Point the way to run!

Who on the brown earth
Knows himself one?
Life is in lichens
That sleep as they run.

Theodore Weiss

A MAGIC CARPET

The butterfly is O flutter by
a Persian wrapt and driven
by a drunken driver,
as though its own fast colors
or its teeter
hour after hour
on all the perchable,
high-
towered
flowers
had intoxicated it.

Or maybe it's the hanging gardens
of Babylon,
a slip of Eden looking
for its way back in again.

So like the ribbon
of a giddy girl
it bobs
and lights
then takes the breeze
and, taking, fans it—
see it blow!—
into a pas de deux.

Never mistake its zigzag flight:
itself is where it wants
to go.

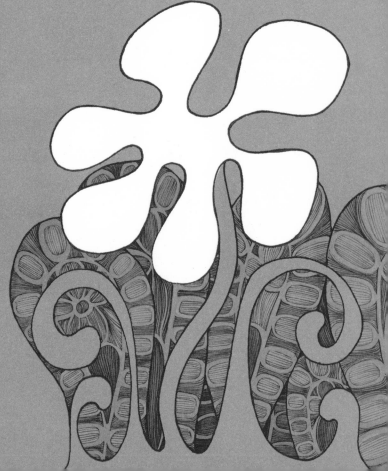

Stanley Kunitz

THE WALTZER IN THE HOUSE

A sweet, a delicate white mouse,
A little blossom of a beast,
Is waltzing in the house
Among the crackers and the yeast.

O the swaying of his legs!
O the bobbing of his head!
The lady, beautiful and kind,
The blue-eyed mistress, lately wed,
Has almost laughed away her wits
To see the pretty mouse that sits
On his tiny pink behind
And swaying, bobbing, begs.

She feeds him tarts and curds,
Seed packaged for the birds,
And figs, and nuts, and cheese;
Polite as Pompadour to please
The dainty waltzer of her house,
The sweet, the delicate, the innocent white mouse.

As in a dream, as in a trance,
She loves his rhythmic elegance,
She laughs to see his bobbing dance.

Robert Frost

FIREFLIES IN THE GARDEN

Here come real stars to fill the upper skies,
And here on earth come emulating flies,
That though they never equal stars in size,
(And they were never really stars at heart)
Achieve at times a very star-like start.
Only, of course, they can't sustain the part.

John Crowe Ransom

LITTLE BOY BLUE

He rubbed his eyes and wound the silver horn.
Then the continuum was cracked and torn
With tumbling imps of music being born.

The blowzy sheep lethargic on the ground
Suddenly burned where no fire could be found
And straight up stood their fleeces every pound.

The old bellwether rose and rang his bell,
The seven-days' lambs went skipping and skipped well,
And Baa Baa Baa, the flock careered pellmell.

The yellow cows that milked the savoury cud
Propped on the green grass or the yellow mud
Felt such a tingle in their lady blood,

They ran and tossed their hooves and horns of blue
And jumped the fence and gambolled kangaroo,
Divinely singing as they wandered Moo.

A plague on such a shepherd of the sheep
That careless boy with pretty cows to keep!
With such a burden I should never sleep.

But when his notes had run around the sky,
When they proceeded to grow faint and die,
He stuffed his horn with straw and put it by.

And when the legs were tired beneath the sheep
And there were spent and sleepy cows to keep,
He rubbed his eyes again and went to sleep.

Wallace Stevens

PLOUGHING ON SUNDAY

The white cock's tail
Tosses in the wind.
The turkey-cock's tail
Glitters in the sun.

Water in the fields.
The wind pours down.
The feathers flare
And bluster in the wind.

Remus, blow your horn!
I'm ploughing on Sunday,
Ploughing North America.
Blow your horn!

Tum-ti-tum.
Ti-tum-tum-tum!
The turkey-cock's tail
Spreads to the sun.

The white cock's tail
Streams to the moon.
Water in the fields.
The wind pours down.

AFTERWORDS

Some years ago while teaching kindergarten in a public school in a small, poor town, I decided to test a favorite theory of mine: that young children would respond to the very best in art. I chose Bach and Beethoven and Bartok to dance to, as well as folk song. Rouault and Picasso clowns lined up beside *Life's* circus photographs and our own Bozo. And Cummings, Frost and Williams echoed in our room along with nursery rhymes. The children in the class were delighted. It occurred to me, as a consequence, that others would be too. Out of the poetry collection I made at that time this present little paper zoo came into being. I have chosen modern American poems because young children, in their usual encounters with poetry, are unlikely to meet them, and because the contemporary language speaks directly to the child. These poems were not written especially for children. However, they were selected in the belief that the young child could enjoy them and continue to grow with them, and that the adult would share with the young child the wide-eyed moments when suddenly "The grass divides" and "A spotted shaft is seen"; or when "The white cock's tail/Tosses in the wind"; or when "a bird singing in a tree...sings till everywhere is here."

Renée Karol Weiss

Much as I would like to say "Let my work speak for itself," I won't. And I can't. The poems may speak for themselves; the illustrator may only interpret what he hears. In this book I consider literal interpretation unfair to the young reader who is learning to visualize abstract words. (At times it could be helpful to read a poem aloud to a child and have him verbalize the picture before he sees my illustration.) What I have attempted to do in my illustrations is to complement the poetry (from ear to eye) and decorate each page. There are sixteen different poets in this book and I have retained one style— free, loose drawings with tight textural decorations. A singular style provides consistency to an anthology; and this particular style, free and tight, to me is poetry.

Ellen Raskin